KT-379-562

MR and Earle —
with love from
Monica — 2008 —
£1·00

VIRGINIA

OOLF

TEXT SELECTION BY JANE DUNN

AURUM PRESS

First published 1994 by Aurum Press Ltd
25 Bedford Avenue, London WC1B 3AT

Conceived, edited and designed by Russell Ash & Bernard Higton

Text selection copyright © 1994 by Jane Dunn
Design copyright © 1994 by Russell Ash & Bernard Higton

All rights reserved. No part of this book may be reproduced or
utilized in any form or by any means, electronic or mechanical, including
photocopying, recording or by any information storage and retrieval
system, without permission in writing from Aurum Press Limited.

A catalogue record for this book is available from the British Library

ISBN 1 85410 325 3

2 4 6 8 10 9 7 5 3 1
1995 1997 1998 1996 1994

Printed in Hong Kong

All quotations are by Virginia Woolf, unless otherwise stated.

తిఏఠ

Tenuousness and purity were in her baptismal name, and a hint of fang in the other.

VITA SACKVILLE-WEST, HORIZON, MAY 1941

Who was I then? Adeline Virginia Stephen...descended from a great many people, some famous, others obscure; born into a large connection, born not of rich parents, but of well-to-do parents, born into a very communicative, literate, letter writing, visiting, articulate late nineteenth-century world...

'A SKETCH OF THE PAST' IN MOMENTS OF BEING

*I*MPRESSIONS OF VIRGINIA

The young ladies – Vanessa was twenty-one or twenty-two, Virginia eighteen or nineteen – were just as formidable as their father, perhaps even more so. I first saw them one summer afternoon in Thoby's rooms; in white dresses and large hats, with parasols in their hands, their beauty literally took one's breath away, for suddenly seeing them one stopped astonished and everything including one's breathing for one second also stopped as it does when in a picture gallery you suddenly come face to face with a great Rembrandt or Velasquez...the observant observer would have noticed at the back of the two Miss Stephens' eyes a look which would have warned him to be cautious, a look which belied the demureness, a look of great intelligence, hypercritical, sarcastic, satirical...It was almost impossible for a man not to fall in love with them, and I think that I did at once.

LEONARD WOOLF, AN AUTOBIOGRAPHY: SOWING

Virginia knows how to be utterly charming if she likes, and today she did. Playing bowls she is the cracked Englishwoman, with an old felt hat on the top of her head and long pointed canvas shoes. She started some way behind the jack, and took a little run and then hurled her bowl with wildly waving arms...I can't describe to you the kindness as well as fascination of everything she said – about the beauty of Ham Spray, about life in the country...I was bowled over by her irresistible cracked charm. Tell Alix [Strachey] she [Virginia] is going to be the newest motor-bicycle addict, for she says Leonard won't let her drive the car and a motor bike is just what she wants.

FRANCES PARTRIDGE, MEMORIES

Virginia Woolf, notably beautiful with a beauty of bone and form and line that belonged to the stars rather than the sun, manifested in her appearance, in spite of the modernity that was clearly there, a Victorian distinction.

OSBERT SITWELL, *LAUGHTER IN THE NEXT ROOM*

The bay was a large lap, many-curved, sand-edged, silver green with sandhills, flowing to the Lighthouse rocks at one end, which made two black stops, one of them with the black and white Lighthouse tower on it. At the other end, the Hayle river made a bar, like a vein across the sand, with the stakes marking the channel, on which the seagulls sat. This great flowing scoop of sea was always changing colour: deep blue; emerald; green; purple; silver. Ships were always steaming in or out: the Haines line, for the most part small steamers going to Cardiff for coal. In rough weather all sorts of tramp steamers came in for shelter – low ships, with a dip in the middle, painted a rusty red. Sometimes a great three-funnelled ship would anchor; and once some famous white yacht. Then there was a perpetual sailing of fishing boats from the Harbour – the luggers, with their sails rigged half across the mast; the rather heavy clumsy boats that went far out, deep sea fishing, and the lighter mackerel boats, that came racing back in the evening, rounding the Island and dropping their sails.

'A SKETCH OF THE PAST' IN *MOMENTS OF BEING*

You have given a portrait of mother which is more like her to me than anything I could ever have conceived possible. It is almost painful to have her so raised from the dead. You have made me feel the extraordinary beauty of her character, which must be the most difficult thing in the world to do.

LETTER FROM VANESSA BELL, 11 MAY 1927

'Yes, of course, if it's fine to-morrow,' said Mrs Ramsay. 'But you'll have to be up with the lark,' she added.

To her son these words conveyed an extraordinary joy, as if it were settled the expedition were bound to take place, and the wonder to which he had looked forward, for years and years it seemed, was, after a night's darkness and a day's sail, within touch...

'But,' said his father, stopping in front of the drawing-room window, 'it won't be fine.'

To the Lighthouse

It is perfectly true that she obsessed me, in spite of the fact that she died when I was thirteen, until I was forty-four. Then one day walking round Tavistock Square I made up, as I sometimes make up my books, *To the Lighthouse*; in a great, apparently involuntary, rush…and when it was written, I ceased to be obsessed by my mother. I no longer hear her voice; I do not see her.

'A SKETCH OF THE PAST' IN *MOMENTS OF BEING*

Silenced, she returned to her private vision; of beauty which is goodness; the sea on which we float. Mostly impervious, but surely every boat sometimes leaks?

He would carry the torch of reason till it went out in the darkness of the cave. For herself, every morning, kneeling, she protected her vision. Every night she opened the window and looked at leaves against the sky. Then slept. Then the random ribbon of birds' voices woke her.

BETWEEN THE ACTS

MRS RAMSAY

She now remembered what she had been going to say about Mrs Ramsay. She did not know how she would have put it; but it would have been something critical. She had been annoyed the other night by some high-handedness. Looking along the level of Mr Bankes's glance at her, she thought that no woman could worship another woman in the way he worshipped; they could only seek shelter under the shade which Mr Bankes extended over them both. Looking along his beam she added to it her different ray, thinking that she was unquestionably the loveliest of people (bowed over her book); the best perhaps; but also, different too from the perfect shape which one saw there. But why different, and how different?...What was the spirit in her, the essential thing, by which, had you found a glove in the corner of a sofa, you would have known it, from its twisted finger, hers indisputably? She was like a bird for speed, an arrow for directness. She was wilful; she was commanding (of course, Lily reminded herself, I am thinking of her relations with women, and I am much younger, an insignificant person, living off the Brompton Road). She opened bedroom windows. She shut doors. (So she tried to start the tune of Mrs Ramsay in her head.) Arriving late at night, with a light tap on one's bedroom door, wrapped in an old fur coat (for the setting of her beauty was always that – hasty, but apt), she would enact again whatever it might be – Charles Tansley losing his umbrella; Mr Carmichael snuffling and sniffing; Mr Bankes saying, 'the vegetable salts are lost'. All this she would adroitly shape; even maliciously twist; and, moving over to the window, in

pretence that she must go, – it was dawn, she could see the sun rising, – half turn back, more intimately, but still always laughing, insist that she must, Minta must, they all must marry, since in the whole world, whatever laurels might be tossed to her (but Mrs Ramsay cared not a fig for her painting), or triumphs won by her (probably Mrs Ramsay had her share of those), and here she saddened, darkened, and came back to her chair, there could be no disputing this: an unmarried woman (she lightly took her hand for a moment), an unmarried woman has missed the best of life.

TO THE LIGHTHOUSE

11

IMPRESSION OF FATHER

I t was a splendid mind. For if thought is like the keyboard of a piano, divided into so many notes, or like the alphabet is ranged in twenty-six letters all in order, then his splendid mind had no sort of difficulty in running over those letters one by one, firmly and accurately, until it had reached, say, the letter Q. He reached Q. Very few people in the whole of England ever reach Q. Here, stopping for one moment by the stone urn which held the geraniums, he saw, but now far far away, like children picking up shells, divinely innocent and occupied with little trifles at their feet and somehow entirely defenceless against a doom which he perceived, his wife and son, together, in the window. They needed his protection; he gave it them. But after Q? What comes next? After Q there are a number of letters the last of which is scarcely visible to mortal eyes, but glimmers red in the distance. Z is only reached once by one man in a generation. Still, if he could reach R it would be something. Here at least was Q. He dug his heels in at Q. Q he was sure of. Q he could demonstrate. If Q then is Q–R – Here he knocked his pipe out, with two or three resonant taps on the ram's horn which made the handle of the urn, and proceeded. 'Then R...' He braced himself. He clenched himself.

Qualities that would have saved a ship's company exposed on a broiling sea with six biscuits and a flask of water – endurance and justice, foresight, devotion, skill, came to his help. R is then – what is R?

...The lizard's eye flickered once more. The veins on his forehead bulged. The geranium in the urn became startlingly visible and, displayed among its leaves, he could see, without wishing it, that old, that obvious distinction between the two classes of men; on the one hand the steady goers of superhuman strength who,

plodding and persevering, repeat the whole alphabet in order, twenty-six letters in all, from start to finish; on the other hand the gifted, the inspired who, miraculously, lump all the letters together in one flash – the way of genius. He had not genius; he laid no claim to that: but he had, or might have had, the power to repeat every letter of the alphabet from A to Z accurately in order. Meanwhile, he stuck at Q. On, then, on to R.

Feelings that would not have disgraced a leader who, now that the snow has begun to fall and the mountain-top is covered in mist, knows that he must lay himself down and die before morning comes, stole upon him, paling the colour of his eyes, giving him, even in the two minutes of his turn on the terrace, the bleached look of withered old age. Yet he would not die lying down; he would find some crag of rock, and there, his eyes fixed on the storm, trying to the end to pierce the darkness, he would die standing. He would never reach R.

To The Lighthouse

13

Social Graces

Our London season about which you ask, was of the dullest description. I only went to three dances – and I think of nothing else. But the truth of it is, as we frequently tell each other, we are failures. Really we can't shine in Society. I don't know how it's done. We ain't popular – we sit in corners and look like mutes who are longing for a funeral.

Letter, 8 August 1901

ℰℐ

I remember the humiliation of standing, unasked, against a wall. I remember of these parties humiliation – I could not dance; frustration – I could not get young men to talk; and also, for happily that good friend has never deserted me – the scene as a spectacle to be described later. And some moments of elation: some moments of lyrical ecstasy. But the pressure of society in 1900 almost forbad any natural feeling.

'A Sketch of the Past' in Moments of Being,

ℰℐ

It was only in silence…that her daughters could sport with infidel ideas which they had brewed for themselves of a life different from hers; in Paris, perhaps; a wilder life; not always taking care of some man or other…

To the Lighthouse

SISTERS: A CLOSE CONSPIRACY

As you have the children, the fame by rights belongs to me.

LETTER TO VANESSA BELL, 2 JUNE 1926

I am sometimes overcome by the finest qualities in her. When she chooses she can give one the most extraordinary sense of bigness of point of view. I think she has in reality amazing courage & sanity about life.

LETTER FROM VANESSA BELL TO ROGER FRY, 24 DECEMBER 1912

There have been no great adventures to speak of, save that the Bridge was open last night as we came through, in a storm of rain, a sailing ship passing, and all very romantic, and as usual I thought of you. Do you think we have the same pair of eyes, only different spectacles? I rather think I'm more nearly attached to you than sisters should be. Why is it I never stop thinking of you, even when walking in the marsh this afternoon and seeing a great snake like a sea serpent gliding among the grass?

LETTER TO VANESSA BELL, 17 AUGUST 1937

There is an atmosphere of undiluted male here. How you would hate it! If only you were here we should now light a fire and sit over it talking the whole morning, with our skirts up to our trousers. You would say 'Now what shall we talk about?' and I if I were tactful would say 'Our past', and then we should begin and discuss all our marvellous past and George's delinquencies, etc., and so come to our present and then on to your future and

whether and whom you should marry, and then at last to the one great subject. 'Now what do you really think of your brains, Billy?' I should say with such genuine interest that you'd have to tell me and we should probably reach the most exalted spheres. Why aren't you here?

LETTER FROM VANESSA BELL, 21 AUGUST 1908

$\mathcal{V}$ANESSA BELL

U nderneath the necklaces and the enamel butterflies was one passionate desire – for paint and turpentine, for turpentine and paint.

(VANESSA BY VIRGINIA) *MOMENTS OF BEING*,
'22 HYDE PARK GATE'

Well, goodbye, my honeybee; Tell me Julian's witticisms. You have a touch in letter writing that is beyond me. Something unexpected, like coming round a corner in a rose garden and finding it still daylight.

LETTER TO VANESSA BELL, 10 AUGUST 1908

I had a charming long letter from you this morning with flattering hints of rose-gardens and daylight round corners and I don't know what all. I purr all down my back when I get such gems of imagery thrown at my feet and reflect how envied I shall be of the world some day when it learns on what terms I was with that great genius…

LETTER FROM VANESSA BELL TO VIRGINIA, 11 AUGUST 1908

The artist's temperament is such a difficult thing to manage and she has volcanoes underneath her sedate manner.

LETTER FROM VIRGINIA ABOUT VANESSA, 22 APRIL 1900

THE COMING OF BLOOMSBURY

These Thursday evening parties were, as far as I'm concerned, the germ from which sprang all that has since come to be called – in newspapers, in novels, in Germany, in France – even, I daresay, in Turkey and Timbuktu – by the name of Bloomsbury. Yet how difficult – how impossible. Talk – even the talk which had such tremendous results upon the lives and characters of the two Miss Stephens – even talk of this interest and importance is as elusive as smoke. It flies up the chimney and is gone.

'OLD BLOOMSBURY' IN *MOMENTS OF BEING*

[Bloomsbury] is like nothing so much as the lions house at the Zoo. One goes from cage to cage. All the animals are dangerous, rather suspicious of each other, and full of fascination and mystery. I'm sometimes too timid to go in, and trail along the pavement, looking in at the windows.

LETTER, 23 DECEMBER 1920

They were a group of rational and liberal individuals with an arduous work ethic and an aristocratic ideal. Each labored in his separate vineyard. They had a passion for art; they liked the full-

ness of life; they knew how to relax when their day's work was done. They wrote. They painted. They decorated. They built furniture. They sat on national committees. They achieved a large fame. They were damnably critical...People who knew them were irritated, and some found them rude and abrasive...To others they were the least boring people in the world, for they had intelligence and charm, though no doubt a certain high and gentry view of civilisation.

LEON EDEL, *A HOUSE OF LIONS*

*F*RIENDSHIP

Yes, they did like each other; also they shared a taste for discussion in the pursuit of truth and contempt for conventional ways of thinking and feeling – contempt for conventional morals if you will. Does it not strike you that as much could be said of many collections of young or youngish people in many ages and many lands?

CLIVE BELL, 'BLOOMSBURY' IN *OLD FRIENDS*

These swarming hot summer days seem to quicken human life as well as vegetable. One becomes a flower oozing honey upon which ones friends cluster – or such is my version of the relationship. This week we've had Ottoline, & Lytton...I need not repeat the stock observations upon his mellow good humour. It is more to the point to chronicle a renewed sense of affection, which has never been seriously in abeyance, & the usual conviction that his wit & what he calls personality are as peculiar to him as his voice, or his finger nails. And then one thinks that it doesn't much matter if his writing is not profound or original; one begins perhaps to suspect that it may be more original than one thinks.

DIARY, 16 MAY 1919

'Love apart, whom would you most like to see coming up the drive?' Lytton asked Clive Bell one rainy afternoon in the depths of the country. Clive Bell hesitated a moment and Lytton replied to his own question: 'Virginia, of course.'

MICHAEL HOLROYD, *LYTTON STRACHEY: A BIOGRAPHY*

Clive Bell: A sort of mixture between Shelley and a sporting country squire. *(Virginia Woolf)*

Maynard Keynes: A kind and even simple heart under that immensely impressive armour of intellect. *(Virginia Woolf)*

Vanessa Bell: The high priestess of Bloomsbury. *(Leon Edel)*

Duncan Grant: So incredibly full of charm, his genius as an artist seems to overflow so into his life & character. *(Vanessa Bell)* Has the rare secret of eternal youth. *(Ottoline Morrell)*

Lytton Strachey: His conversation is always fascinating and instructive. He is kind and sympathetic, intolerant and prejudiced to a degree. *(Dora Carrington)*

Virginia Woolf: Virginia is I believe a more simple character than appears on the surface…Her cleverness is so great that one doesn't at first see a kind of ingenuousness of feeling underneath. *(Lytton Strachey)*

Roger Fry: An absolutely enthralling companion…such sympathy…such fascinating speculations and trains of thought seemed to spring continually from some inexhaustible source. *(Vanessa Bell)*

Desmond MacCarthy: Who is more tolerant, more appreciative, more understanding of human nature? *(Virginia Woolf)*

Adrian Stephen: He wilted, pale under a stone of vivacious brothers & sisters. *(Virginia Woolf)*

Saxon Sydney-Turner: It was easy to believe he was a genius; but it was easier still to believe that his genius would never result in anything positive. *(Quentin Bell)*

Ｌeonard Woolf

I've got a confession to make. I'm going to marry Leonard Wolf [sic]. He's a penniless Jew. I'm more happy than anyone ever said was possible – but I insist on your liking him too.

LETTER, FROM VIRGINIA TO VIOLET DICKINSON, 4 JUNE 1912

Dearest Mongoose, darling Mongoose,
I am writing in a field overlooking Burgundy; 4.30: very hot and fine…I am now getting melancholy for you, and thinking perhaps the downs are more beautiful than Burgundy…I don't think I could stand more than a week away from you, as there are so many things to say to you, which I cant say to Vita – though she is most sympathetic and more intelligent than you think…Poor Mandril [herself] does adore every hair of your little body and hereby puts in a claim for an hour of antelope kissing the moment she gets back.

LETTER TO LEONARD WOOLF, 25 SEPTEMBER 1928

His being seemed conglobulated in his brow, his lips were pressed; his eyes were fixed, but suddenly they flashed with laughter. Also he suffered from chilblains, the penalty of an

imperfect circulation. Unhappy, unfriended, in exile...Yes, but we were also quick to perceive how cutting, how apt, how severe he was, how naturally, when we lay under the elm trees pretending to watch cricket, we awaited his approval, seldom given...He remained aloof; enigmatic; a scholar capable of that inspired accuracy which has something formidable about it. My phrases (how to describe the moon) did not meet with his approval.

THE WAVES

Leonard thinks less well of me for powdering my nose and spending money on dress. Never mind, I adore Leonard.

DIARY, 26 MAY 1924

*L*OVE

The letter lay upon the hall table; Florinda coming in that night took it up with her, put it on the table as she kissed Jacob, and Jacob seeing the hand, left it there under the lamp, between the biscuit-tin and the tobacco-box. They shut the bedroom door behind them…

These old houses are only brick and wood, soaked in human sweat, grained with human dirt. But if the pale blue envelope lying by the biscuit-box had the feelings of a mother, the heart was torn by the little creak, the sudden stir. Behind the door was the obscene thing, the alarming presence, and terror would come over her as at death, or the birth of a child. Better, perhaps, burst in and face it than sit in the antechamber listening to the little creak, the sudden stir, for her heart was swollen, and pain threaded it. My son, my son – such would be her cry, uttered to hide her vision of him stretched with Florinda, inexcusable, irrational, in a woman with three children living in Scarborough. And the fault lay with Florinda. Indeed, when the door opened and the couple came out, Mrs Flanders would have flounced upon her – only it was Jacob who came first, in his dressing-gown, amiable, authoritative, beautifully healthy, like a baby after an airing, with an eye clear as running water. Florinda followed, lazily stretching;

yawning a little; arranging her hair at the looking-glass – while Jacob read his mother's letter.

JACOB'S ROOM

❧

So that is marriage, Lily thought, a man and a woman looking at a girl throwing a ball.

TO THE LIGHTHOUSE

'Oh, Flush!' said Miss Barrett. For the first time she looked him in the face. For the first time Flush looked at the lady lying on the sofa.

Each was surprised. Heavy curls hung down on each side of Miss Barrett's face; large bright eyes shone out; a large mouth smiled. Heavy ears hung down on each side of Flush's face; his eyes, too, were large and bright: his mouth was wide. There was a likeness between them. As they gazed at each other each felt: Here am I – and then each felt: But how different! Hers was the pale worn face of an invalid, cut off from air, light, freedom. His was the ruddy face of a young animal; instinct with health and energy. Broken asunder, yet made in the same mould, could it be that each completed what was dormant in the other?...Between them lay the widest gulf that can separate one being from another. She spoke. He was dumb. She was woman; he was dog. Thus closely united, thus immensely divided, they gazed at each other. Then with one bound Flush sprang on to the sofa and laid himself where he was to lie for ever after – on the rug at Miss Barrett's feet...

Flush, watching Miss Barrett, saw the colour rush into her face; saw her eyes brighten and her lips open.

'Mr Browning!' she exclaimed.

Twisting his yellow gloves in his hands, blinking his eyes, well groomed, masterly, abrupt, Mr Browning strode across the room. He seized Miss Barrett's hand, and sank into the chair by the sofa at her side. Instantly they began to talk.

What was horrible to Flush, as they talked, was his loneliness.

Once he had felt that he and Miss Barrett were together, in a fire-lit cave. Now the cave was no longer firelit; it was dark and damp; Miss Barrett was outside.

FLUSH

ORLANDO

Yesterday morning I was in despair...I couldn't screw a word from me; and at last dropped my head in my hands: dipped my pen in the ink, and wrote these words, as if automatically, on a clean sheet: Orlando: A Biography. No sooner had I done this than my body was flooded with rapture and my brain with ideas. I wrote rapidly til 12...But listen; suppose Orlando turns out to be Vita...

LETTER TO VITA SACKVILLE-WEST, 9 OCTOBER 1927

It is enough for us to state the simple fact; Orlando was a man until the age of thirty; when he became a woman and has remained so ever since.

ORLANDO

But there she lay content. The scent of the bog myrtle and the meadow-sweet was in her nostrils. The rooks' hoarse laughter was in her ears. 'I have found my mate,' she murmured. 'It is the moor. I am nature's bride,' she whispered, giving herself in rapture to the cold embraces of the grass as she lay folded in her cloak in the hollow by the pool. 'Here will I lie. (A feather fell upon her brow.) I have found a greener laurel than the bay. My forehead will be cool always. There are wild birds' feathers – the owl's, the nightjar's. I shall dream wild dreams. My hands shall wear no wedding ring,' she continued, slipping it from her finger. 'The roots shall twine about them. Ah!' she sighed, pressing her head luxuriously on its spongy pillow, 'I have sought happiness through many ages and not found it; fame and missed it; love and not known it; life – and behold, death is better. I have known many men and many women,' she continued; 'none have I under-

stood. It is better that I should lie at peace here with only the sky above me...'

ORLANDO

You have invented a new form of Narcissism, – I confess, – I am in love with Orlando – this is a complication I had not foreseen. Virginia, my dearest, I can only thank you for pouring out such riches.

LETTER FROM VITA SACKVILLE-WEST, 11 OCTOBER 1928

'WE ARE THE WORDS; WE ARE THE MUSIC; WE ARE THE THING ITSELF'

It is the rapture I get when in writing I seem to be discovering what belongs to what; making a scene come right; making a character come together. From this I reach what I might call a philosophy; at any rate it is a constant idea of mine; that behind the cotton wool is hidden a pattern; that we – I mean all human beings – are connected with this; that the whole world is a work of art; that we are all parts of the work of art. *Hamlet* or a Beethoven quartet is the truth about this vast mass that we call the world. But there is no Shakespeare, there is no Beethoven; certainly and emphatically there is no God; we are the words; we are the music; we are the thing itself.

'A SKETCH OF THE PAST' IN *MOMENTS OF BEING*

Life is not a series of gig lamps symmetrically arranged; life is a luminous halo, a semi-transparent envelope surrounding us from the beginning of consciousness to the end.

'MODERN FICTION' IN *THE COMMON READER*

The bells had stopped; the audience had gone; also the actors. She could straighten her back. She could open her arms. She could say to the world. You have taken my gift! Glory possessed her – for one moment. But what had she given? A cloud that melted into the other clouds on the horizon. It was in the giving that the triumph was. And the triumph faded. If they had understood her meaning; if they had known their parts; if the pearls had been real and the funds illimitable – it would have been a better gift. Now it had gone to join the others.

BETWEEN THE ACTS

'A WOMAN MUST HAVE MONEY AND A ROOM OF HER OWN IF SHE IS TO WRITE FICTION'

I discovered that if I were to review books I should need to do battle with a certain phantom. And the phantom was a woman...you may not know what I mean by the Angel in the House. I will describe her as shortly as I can. She was intensely sympathetic. She was immensely charming. She was utterly unselfish. She excelled in the difficult arts of family life. She sacrificed herself daily. If there was chicken, she took the leg; if there was a draught she sat in it – in short she was so constituted that she never had a mind or a wish of her own, but preferred to sympathize always with the minds and wishes of others. Above all – I need not say it – she was pure. Her purity was supposed to be her chief beauty – her blushes, her great grace. In those days – the last of Queen Victoria – every house had its Angel. And when I came to write I encountered her with the very first words. The shadow of her wings fell on my page; I heard the rustling of her skirts in the room. Directly, that is to say, I took my pen in my hand to review that novel by a famous man, she slipped behind me and whispered: 'My dear, you are a young woman. You are writing about a book that has been written by a 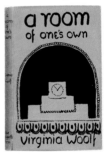 man. Be sympathetic; be tender; flatter; deceive; use all the arts and wiles of our sex. Never let anybody guess that you have a mind of your own. Above all, be pure.' And she made as if to guide my pen. I now record the one act for which I take some credit to myself, though the credit rightly belongs to some excellent ancestors of mine who left me a certain sum of money – shall we say five hundred pounds a year? – so that it was not necessary for me to depend solely on charm for my living. I turned upon her and caught her by the throat. I did my best to kill her. My excuse, if I were to be had up in a court of law, would be that I acted in self-defence. Had I not killed her she would have killed me. She would have plucked the heart out of my writing.

'PROFESSIONS FOR WOMEN' IN *THE DEATH OF THE MOTH AND OTHER ESSAYS*

'*T*HESE GLOOMS'

S he lay in bed, listening to the birds singing in Greek and imagining that King Edward VII lurked in the azaleas using the foulest possible language.

QUENTIN BELL, VIRGINIA WOOLF: A BIOGRAPHY

As an experience, madness is terrific I can assure you, and not to be sniffed at; and in its lava I still find most of the things I write about. It shoots out of one everything shaped, final, not in mere driblets as sanity does. And the six months – not three – that I lay in bed taught me a good deal about what is called oneself.

LETTER TO ETHEL SMYTH, 22 JUNE 1930

But it is always a question whether I wish to avoid these glooms. In part they are the result of getting away by oneself, & having a psychological interest which the usual state of working & enjoying lacks. These 9 weeks give one a plunge into deep waters; which is a little alarming, but full of interest. All the rest of the year one's (I daresay rightly) curbing & controlling this odd immeasurable soul. When it expands, though one is frightened & bored & gloomy, it is as I say to myself, awfully queer. There is an edge to it which I feel of great importance, once in a way. One goes down into the well & nothing protects one from the assault of truth. Down there I cant write or read; I exist however. I am.

DIARY, 28 SEPTEMBER 1926

And if we didn't live venturously, plucking the wild goat by the beard, & trembling over precipices, we should never be depressed, I've no doubt; but already should be faded, fatalistic & aged.

DIARY, 2 AUGUST 1924

'Twice His Natural Size'

Women have served all these centuries as looking-glasses possessing the magic and delicious power of reflecting the figure of man at twice its natural size…That serves to explain in part the necessity that women so often are to men. And it serves to explain how restless they are under her criticism; how impossible it is for her to say to them this book is bad, this picture is feeble, or whatever it may be, without giving far more pain and rousing far more anger than a man would do who gave the same criticism. For if she begins to tell the truth, the figure in the looking-glass shrinks; his fitness for life is diminished. How is he to go on giving judgement, civilising natives, making laws, writing books, dressing up and speechifying at banquets, unless he can see himself at breakfast and at dinner at least twice the size he really is?

A Room of One's Own

Highbrow and Lowbrow

Now there can be no two opinions as to what a highbrow is. He is the man or woman of thoroughbred intelligence who rides his mind at a gallop across country in pursuit of an idea. That is why I have always been so proud to be called highbrow. That is why if I could be more of a highbrow I would. I honour and respect highbrows. Some of my relations have been highbrows; and some, by no means all, of my friends. To be a highbrow, a complete and representative highbrow, a highbrow like Shakespeare, Dickens, Byron, Shelley, Keats, Charlotte Brönte, Scott, Jane Austen, Flaubert, Hardy or Henry James – to name a few highbrows from the same profession chosen at random – is of course beyond the wildest dreams of my imagination. And, though I would cheerfully lay myself down in the dust and kiss the print of their feet, no person of sense will deny that this passionate preoccupation of theirs – riding across country in the pursuit of ideas – often leads to disaster. Undoubtedly, they come fearful croppers...

I need not further labour the point that highbrows, for some reason or other, are wholly incapable of dealing successfully with what is called real life. That is why, and here I come to a point that is often surprisingly ignored, they honour so wholeheartedly and depend so completely upon those who are called lowbrows. By a lowbrow is meant of course a man or woman of thoroughbred vitality who rides his body in pursuit of living at a gallop across life. That is why I honour and respect lowbrows – and I have never known a highbrow who did not. In so far as I am a highbrow (and my imperfections in that line are well known to me) I love lowbrows; I study them; I always sit next the conductor in an omnibus and try to get him to tell me what it is like – being a

conductor. In whatever company I am I always try to know what it is like – being a conductor, being a woman with ten children and thirty-five shillings a week, being a stockbroker, being an admiral, being a bank clerk, being a dressmaker, being a duchess, being a miner, being a cook, being a prostitute. All that lowbrows do is of surpassing interest and wonder to me, because, in so far as I am a highbrow, I cannot do things myself.

DEATH OF THE MOTH AND OTHER ESSAYS

'The Passion of my Life':
Virginia in London

For having lived in Westminster – how many years now? over twenty, – one feels even in the midst of the traffic, or waking at night, Clarissa was positive, a particular hush, or solemnity; an indescribable pause; a suspense (but that might be her heart, affected, they said, by influenza) before Big Ben strikes. There! Out it boomed. First a warning, musical; then the hour, irrevocable. The leaden circles dissolve in the air. Such fools we are, she thought, crossing Victoria Street. For Heaven only knows why one loves it so, how one sees it so, making it up, building it round one, tumbling it, creating it every moment afresh; but the veriest frumps, the most dejected of miseries sitting on doorsteps (drink their downfall) do the same; can't be dealt with, she felt positive, by Acts of Parliament for that very reason: they love life. In people's eyes, in the swing, tramp, and trudge; in the bellow and the uproar; the carriages, motor cars, omnibuses, vans, sandwich men shuffling and swinging; brass bands; barrel organs; in the triumph and the jingle and the strange high singing of some aeroplane overhead was what she loved; life; London; this moment in June.

Mrs Dalloway

The passion of my life, that is the City of London – to see London all blasted, that…raked my heart.

Letter to Ethel Smyth, 11 September 1940

The proximity of the omnibuses gave the outside passengers an opportunity to stare into each other's faces. Yet few took advantage of it. Each had his own business to think of. Each had his past shut in him like the leaves of a book known to him by heart...

JACOB'S ROOM

THE HOGARTH PRESS

Our press arrived on Tuesday. We unpacked it with enormous excitement, finally with Nelly's help, carried it into the drawing room, set it on its stand – and discovered it was smashed in half!…One has great blocks of type, which have to be divided into their separate letters, and founts…We get so absorbed we can't stop; I see that real printing will devour one's entire life…

LETTER TO VANESSA, 26 APRIL 1917

Now the point of the Press is that it entirely prevents brooding, & gives me something solid to fall back on. Anyhow, if I can't write, I can make other people write: I can build up a business.

DIARY, 2 AUGUST 1924

For the first time we have made over £400 profit. And 7 people now depend on us; & I think with pride that 7 people depend, largely, upon my hand writing on a sheet of paper. That is of course a great solace & pride to me. It's not scribbling; its keeping 7 people fed & housed: a great big man like Percy; a carrot faced woman like Cartwright; they live on my words.

DIARY, 13 APRIL 1929

Her hair was allowed to drift about in all directions, she never wore any make-up – she seemed quite devoid of personal vanity, and yet she never appeared anything but beautiful. Sometimes in the summer when I was working in the printing room she'd wander in and set up type or distribute it with her quick, sensitive fingers, looking like a dishevelled angel – her feet bare shuffling about in bedroom slippers, in a nightdress with a great tear down the side, and a dressing-gown vaguely thrown over it, but her mind far, far away from her mechanical task...

PORTRAIT OF VIRGINIA WOOLF, RALPH PARTRIDGE, BBC

Charleston is as usual. One hears Clive shouting in the garden before one arrives. Nessa emerges from a great variegated quilt of asters & artichokes; not very cordial; a little absent-minded...Then Duncan drifts in, also vague, absent minded, & incredibly wrapped round with yellow waistcoats, spotted ties, & old blue stained painting jackets. His trousers have to be hitched up constantly. He rumples his hair. However I can't help thinking that we grow in cordiality, instead of drifting out of sight...

DIARY, 26 AUGUST 1922

We are at Rodmell on the loveliest spring day: soft: a blue veil in the air torn by birds voices. I am glad to be alive & sorry for the dead...

DIARY, 24 MARCH 1932

And so to Rodmell for the week end & the bees buzzing in the hyacinths: the earth emerging very chastened and sharpened from winter under a veil; which became fog as

we drove up, & is fog again today. In addition the house rings with the clamour of electricians: the new bath engine being inserted; & then the Surveyor comes & says we are weighting the floors down with books: a heavy bill threatens; so out to buy ink for my new Waterman, with which I am to take notes for a new Common Reader; & Ethel Sands to tea – my first visitor.

DIARY, 14 FEBRUARY 1934

Green is the colour that comes to mind when I think of the house and garden, with its curling fig trees and level expanse of lawn overlooking the water-meadows. Green was Virginia's colour; a green crystal pear stood always on the table in the sitting-room, symbol of her personality.

ANGELICA GARNETT, *DECEIVED WITH KINDNESS*

Then I had the vision, in Aegina, of an uncivilised, hot new season to be brought into our lives – how yearly we shall come here, with a tent, escaping England, & sloughing the respectable skin; & all the tightness & formality of London; & fame, & wealth; & go back & become irresponsible, livers, existing on bread yoat, butter, eggs, say in Crete. This is to some extent a genuine impulse, I thought, coming down the hill with easy strides; London is not enough, nor Sussex either. One wants to be sunbaked, & taken back to these loquacious friendly people, simply to live, to talk, not to read & write. And then I looked up and saw the mountains across the bay, knife shaped, coloured, & the sea, brimming, smooth; & felt as if a knife had scraped some incrusted organ in me, for I could not find anything lacking in

that agile, athletic beauty, steeped in colour, so that it was not cold, perfectly free from vulgarity, yet old in human life, so that every inch has its wild flower that might grow in an English garden, & the peasants are gentle people; & their clothes, worn & burnt, are subtly coloured, though coarse. Now there are sympathies between people & places, as between human beings. And I could love Greece, as an old woman, so I think, as I once loved Cornwall, as a child.

DIARY, 8 MAY 1932

$\mathcal{A}$T WAR

How England consoles & warms one, in these deep hollows,where the past stands almost stagnant. And the little spire across the fields...so back through Lewes. And I worshipped the beauty of the country, now scraped, but with old colours showing.

DIARY, 24 DECEMBER 1940

Ought I not to look at the sunset rather than write this? A flush or red in the blue; the haystack in the marsh catches the glow; behind me, the apples are red in the trees. L. is gathering them. Now a plume of smoke goes from the train under [Mount] Caburn. And all the air a solemn stillness holds til 8.30 when the cadaverous twanging in the sky begins; the planes going to London. Well its an hour to that. Cows feeding. The elm tree sprinkling its little leaves against the sky. Our pear tree swagged with pears; & the weathercock above the triangular church tower above it...Last night a great heavy plunge of bombs under the window. So near we both started. A plane had passed dropping this fruit. We went on to the terrace. Trinkets of stars sprinkled & glittering. All quiet...Caburn was crowned with what looked like a settled moth, wings extended – a Messerschmitt it was, shot down on Sunday.

DIARY, 2 OCTOBER 1940

' *T*HE PLUNGE INTO DEEP WATERS'

Dearest,
   I want to tell you that you have given me complete happiness. No one could have done more than you have done. Please believe that.

But I know that I shall not get over this: and I am wasting your life. It is this madness. Nothing anyone says can persuade me. You can work, and you will be much better without me. You see I can't write this even, which shows I am right. All I want to say is that until this disease came on we were perfectly happy. It was all due to you. No one could have been so good as you have been, from the very first day till now. Everyone knows that. V.

LAST LETTER, TO LEONARD WOOLF, 28 MARCH 1941

Leonard told me that there are two great elms at Rodmell which she always called Leonard and Virginia. They grow together by the pond. He is going to bury her ashes under one and have a tablet on the tree, with a quotation – the one about 'Death is the enemy. Against you I will fling myself, unvanquished and unyielding. O Death!' [the last lines of *The Waves*]…Poor Leonard – he did break down completely when he told me. He was afraid I'd think him sentimental but it seems so appropriate that I could only think it right.

LETTER FROM VANESSA BELL TO VITA SACKVILLE-WEST, 29 APRIL 1941

Against you I will fling myself, unvanquished
and unyielding, O Death!

PICTURE CREDITS

Bridgeman Art Library: front jacket btm left (© Estate of Dame Laura Knight, reproduced by permission of Curtis Brown Group), back jacket top, 8 (*Forbes Magazine* Collection), 18, 45 (Bradford Art Gallery and Museum), 51 (© Estate of Mrs G.A. Wyndham-Lewis); Charleston Trust: back jacket btm, 49; Christie's Images: 3; Anthony d'Offay Gallery: 11, 19, 20, 23, 24, 25, 28, 36, 50; Fine Art Photographs: 39, 52–53; John Hillelson Agency: 34 and 55 (photos Dr Giselle Freund); Hulton Deutsch: front jacket, 13, 14; Marshall Cavendish: 37, 46; National Portrait Gallery: 37, 43; National Trust: back jacket centre (Eric Crichton), 5, 9 (Eric Crichton), 21 (Roy Fox), 48; Portsmouth City Museums: 29; Private collection: 6 (on loan to Penzance District Museum), 7, 17, 26; Sotheby's: 47, 56; John Ward: 41.

Paintings by Vanessa Bell appear on pages 3, 5, 11, 20, 23, 27, 28, 31, 47, 48, 49, and back jacket centre and btm.

The work of Duncan Grant (paintings on pages 18, 19, 21, 24, 25, and 29) is © Estate of Duncan Grant 1978.

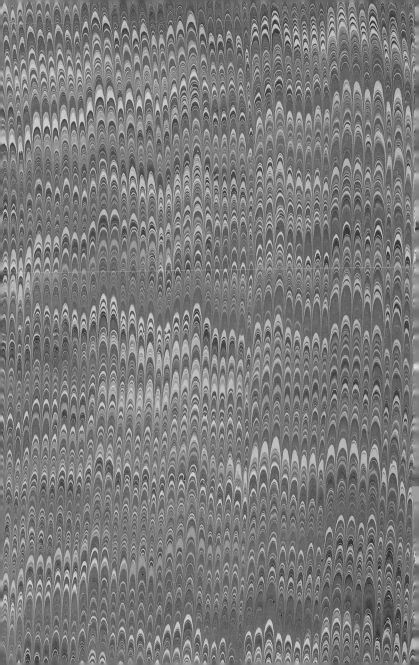